The hardest battle to win i life is the one against your mind. Your brain can't always distinguish between reality and imagination, so if you're not careful with your thoughts, you'll eventually lose your mind. No matter where you are in life, the content of this book will help you overcome your struggles, providing a foundation to strengthen your subconscious mind and take control of your future. You're reading this book because you want more from yourself —maintain that mindset, and success will be inevitable.

Contents

Day 1: Loneliness	3
Day 2: Victory	6
Day 3: Worthiness	9
Day 4: Voids	12
Day 5: Healthy	15
Day 6: Noncoincidence	18
Day 7: Anxiety	21
Day 8: Prayer	24
Day 9: Faith	27
Day 10: Affirm	30
Day 11: Give	33
Day 12: Love	36
Day 13: Self-love	39
Day 14: Humility	42
Day 15: Learn	45
Day 16: Childish	48
Day 17: Failure	51
Day 18: Respect	54
Day 19: Light	57
Day 20: Bandwagon	60
Day 21: Relentless	63
Day 22: Believe	66
Day 23: Environment	69
Day 24: Try	72
Day 25: Hardship	75
Day 26: Pain	78
Day 27: Family	81
Day 28: Vision	84
Day 29: Gratitude	87
Day 30: Valuable	90

Day 1
Loneliness

Loneliness is your strength. When you feel alone, your weakness becomes your superpower. Every hero must walk their path alone. When Jesus went to the Mount of Olives before His crucifixion, He was alone. When you are in alignment with your purpose, God will purposely place you in solitude.

'For my father and my mother have forsaken me, but the Lord will take me in.' Psalm 27:10

My Day 1

Express yourself

Day 2

Victory

You are a victor, not a victim. It's easy to live in victimhood and blame the past for our misfortunes. Taking accountability for your emotions and moving forward can be challenging, but it's essential. You can't change the past, but you can start today to create a better future.

'No, in all these things we are more than conquerors through him who loved us.'
Romans 8:37

My Day 2

You are what you think

Day 3
Worthy

You are worthy of all good things. The world is quick to write you off because of past mistakes, but you must give yourself grace to grow. Surround yourself with people who can see the good in you. Anyone who refuses to see you in a positive light after you've done the work to change is simply seeking a sense of moral superiority. Their ego drives them to feel better about themselves by projecting you as a bad individual.

'For by grace you have been saved through faith. And this is not your own doing; it is the gift of God'
Ephesians 2:8

My Day 3

What are you worthy of?

Day 4
Voids

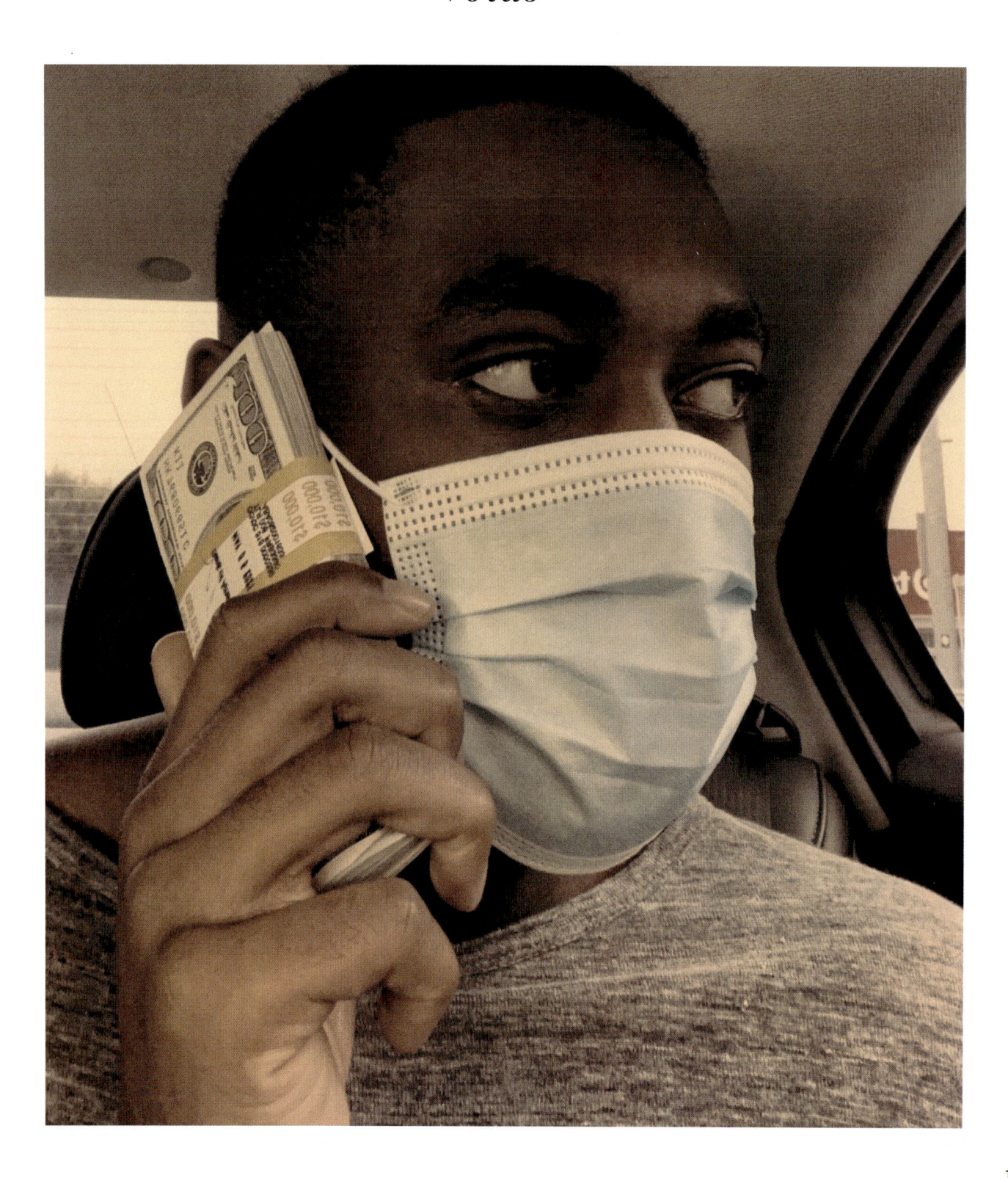

God completes you. No amount of money, sex, or drugs can fill your void—only God can. You can't run from the pain; embrace your emotions and let them flow through you. Some days will be better than others, but as long as you keep trying, one day everything will work itself out.

'But seek first the kingdom of God and his righteousness, and all these things will be added to you.' Matthew 6:33

My Day 4

What are your voids?

Day 5

Healthy

Healthy is wealthy. A high-earning career with a low-quality life is a miserable combination. To be well-off, you must be fortified mentally, physically, spiritually, emotionally, and financially. As Pharrell said, "Wealth is of the heart and mind, not the pocket."

'If anyone destroys God's temple, God will destroy him. For God's temple is holy, and you are that temple.' 1 Corinthians 3:17

My Day 5

Excercise your thoughts here

Day 6

Noncoincidence

All things are working together for your good. You are in the right place at the right time. It's not happening to you; it's happening for you. Regardless of the outcome, the results are the best thing that can possibly happen to you in that moment.

'And we know that for those who love God all things work together for good, for those who are called according to his purpose.' Romans 8:28

My Day 6

Energy flows where attetion goes

Day 7

Anxiety

Don't be anxious about anything. Everything will be okay in the end, and if it's not, then it means you're not at the end yet. Don't worry—God's got it, in His time.

'Look at the birds of the air: they neither sow nor reap nor gather into barns, and yet your heavenly Father feeds them. Are you not of more value than they?' Matthew 6:26

My Day 7

You have a license to just chill

Day 8

Pray

Pray about anything and everything. The answers you seek are just one prayer away. Prayer changes things. One of my favorite songs is "Prayer Changes Things" by Deitrick Haddon, and he sings a powerful verse: "More prayer, more power; less prayer, less power."

'Pray without ceasing.' 1 Thesssalonians 5:17

My Day 8

Write a prayer

Day 9
Faith

Have faith, no matter the circumstance. Life is about surviving the storms, and each one shall pass. It's always darkest before dawn.

'Weeping may endure for a night, but joy comes in the morning' Psalm 30:5

My Day 9

Conquer your doubts

Day 10

Affirm

You will live and not die. Speak life into everything you do. If you keep claiming and believing that life is good, even when it's not, eventually it will be again. Our subconscious is powerful, but you must be intentional with your thoughts to unlock its full potential.

'Death and life are in the power of the tongue, and those who love it will eat its fruits.' Proverbs 18:21

My Day 10

Write 10 affirmations and repeat them daily

Day 11
Give

Blessings lie in giving, not receiving. To gain, you must lose. God honors a cheerful giver.

'One gives freely, yet grows all the richer; another withholds what he should give, and only suffers want.' Proverbs 11:24

My Day 11

How can you selflessly give more?

Day 12

Love

To love is to live. It's a risk worth the odds. Don't be afraid to experience the most beautiful aspect of living.

'A new commandment I give to you, that you love one another: just as I have loved you, you also are to love one another.' John 13:34

My Day 12

Who do you love?

Day 13

Self-love

Love yourself more than anyone else. How can you properly love others if you don't even love yourself? Protect your star player—you.

'Let no one despise you for your youth, but set the believers an example in speech, in conduct, in love, in faith, in purity.' 1 Timothy 4:12

My Day 13
Do something nice for yourself today

Day 14
Humility

Humility comes before honor. Before you rise, you must fall. Consider it the rite of passage in a hero's journey.

'Before destruction a man's heart is haughty, but humility comes before honor.' Proverbs 18:12

My Day 14

Anything humbling you at the moment?

Day 15

Learn

The more you learn, the more people you can help. No one will care more about your community than you. Therefore, you owe it to them to gain as much knowledge as possible to better address socioeconomic issues.

'How much better to get wisdom than gold! To get understanding is to be chosen rather than silver.'
Proverbs 16:16

My Day 15

Educate yourself

Day 16

Childish

Make the kid in you proud. Keep a childlike imagination, because that is the lifeblood of dreams. When you lose your childishness, your dreams will die. Dream, baby, dream.

'In the morning sow your seed, and at evening withhold not your hand, for you do not know which will prosper, this or that, or whether both alike will be good.' Ecclesiastes 11:6

My Day 16

Write a letter to your childhood self

Day 17
Failure

You're failing your way to success. Those weren't setbacks; they were setups. Remember, all things work together for your good.

'For the righteous falls seven times and rises again, but the wicked stumble in times of calamity.' Proverbs 24:16

My Day 17

Turn that L into a W

Day 18
Respect

Respect is greater than money. Not all money is good money, and sacrificing your character in pursuit of riches is vanity. Respect will open more doors than money ever will.

'For what will it profit a man if he gains the whole world and forfeits his soul? Or what shall a man give in return for his soul?'
Matthew 16:26

My Day 18

Treat the doorman like the CEO

Day 19

Light

The world is dark enough as it is—don't lose your light. It's easy to lose hope in society, but God placed you on this earth to do something special. No matter how much chaos you endure, don't forget to keep a pure heart.

'Not only that, but we rejoice in our sufferings, knowing that suffering produces endurance, and endurance produces character, and character produces hope' Romans 5:3-4

My Day 19
Let it shine

Day 20

Bandwagon

Nobody loves you until everybody loves you. You don't need supporters; everyone will want to support you once you become successful. Cheer for yourself until your dreams come true, and don't be surprised when everyone else decides to cheer for you too. Artists often aren't appreciated until years after their work is released. Vincent van Gogh's art didn't become popular until after he died.

'I can do all things through him who strengthens me.'
Phillippians 4:13

My Day 20

You got this

Day 21
Relentless

Go get it. The only person holding you back is yourself. Be relentless until you have it.

'And let us not grow weary of doing good, for in due season we will reap, if we do not give up.' Galatians 6:9

My Day 21

I will not stop until I win

Day 22
Believe

Anything is possible when you believe. All you need is a small seed of faith, and you can accomplish your wildest dreams. Every day, remind yourself that you believe in yourself and your vision— even when you don't.

'Jesus said to him, "Have you believed because you have seen me? Blessed are those who have not seen and yet have believed.'
John 20:29

My Day 22

Don't stop believing

Day 23

Environment

You are a reflection of your environiment. Be mindful of your partner, friends, and workspace. Don't let your surroundings make you complacent. Surround yourself with ambitious individuals, and you'll always be motivated to work on yourself.

'Do not be deceived: Bad company ruins good morals.' 1 Corinthians 15:33

My Day 23
Choose wisely

Day 24

Try

Trying is hard, but regret is harder. In 30 years, you won't care if you tried an idea and it failed, but you will regret never giving yourself a chance to succeed. The burden of untapped potential will haunt you for a lifetime.

'Have I not commanded you? Be strong and courageous. Do not be frightened, and do not be dismayed, for the Lord your God is with you wherever you go.' Joshua 1:9

My Day 24

You're one opportunity away

Day 25
Hardship

Embrace hardship, for without it, growth cannot exist. The biggest blessings always come after the greatest struggles. Be grateful when opposition arises, because it means a successful moment is soon approaching.

'Count it all joy, my brothers, when you meet trials of various kinds, for you know that the testing of your faith produces steadfastness.' James 1:2-3

My Day 25

Let's get it

Day 26

Pain

Turn pain into gain. Suffering is the recipe for success. Your most inspiring work will be a byproduct of the painful moments in your life.

'For I consider that the sufferings of this present time are not worth comparing with the glory that is to be revealed to us.'
Romans 8:18

My Day 26

Let it flow

Day 27
Family

Nothing is more important than family. Money doesn't matter when those you love aren't here to enjoy it with you. God will always bless you abundantly when you honor your family.

'But if anyone does not provide for his relatives, and especially for members of his household, he has denied the faith and is worse than an unbeliever.'
1 Timothy 5:8

My Day 27

Protect the legacy

Day 28

Vision

Have a clear and concise vision. A double-minded person is unstable in all their ways. Without a vision, you will perish.

'Where there is no prophetic vision the people cast off restraint, but blessed is he who keeps the law.' Proverbs 29:18

My Day 29

Write your vision

Day 29

Gratitude

You matter. It's your responsibility to teach others that they matter, too. Don't forget to smile—the world is yours.

'The Lord appeared to him from far away. I have loved you with an everlasting love; therefore I have continued my faithfulness to you.' Jeremiah 31:3

My Day 29
:)

Day 30

Valuable

Be grateful. We often get so wrapped up in what we lack that we forget to appreciate what we have. When you show gratitude for even the smallest things, you'll begin to notice the abundance in your life.

'Give thanks in all circumstances; for this is the will of God in Christ Jesus for you.' 1 Thessalonians 5:18

My Day 30

Finish the mission

Made in the USA
Las Vegas, NV
04 May 2025